Coup D'etat defined

Cayton Thyne and Jonathan Powell's dataset of coups defines attempted coups as "illegal and overt attempts by the military or other elites within the state apparatus to unseat the sitting executive." according to wikipedia

This explains what has been going on from the day President Trump got into office.

If you want a hard copy of facts that you can turn to when someone tells you Trump lies this is the book for you. I have done the research for you and put it down. There is so much more so maybe another book is needed.

President Trump had this to say in a meeting February 28, 2018

"*You take Puls nightclub. If you had one person in that room that could carry a gun and knew how to use it, it wouldn't have happened, or certainly to the extent that it did.*"

The backlash even from the National Rifle Association was alcohol and guns to not mix.

Our President responded with;
@realDonaldTrump

"*When I said that if, within the Orlando club, you had some people with guns. i was obviously talking about additional guards or employees*" June 20, 2016

First off I like that our President is concerned about gays in a nightclub.

This is one way that shows Trump is not a racist

Brandon Straka a New York City hairstylist who happens to be gay realized that the Democratic Party of today use "misinformation and intimidation" to influence. He started the #walkaway movement and as of this date 100,000 have joined and you can see their videos on you tube. FYI if someone tells you the walk away movement was started by Russia they are simply not caught up on current events. You can see more about Brandon Straka on his fa Facebook page.

The next thing to note is even though President Trump was misunder stood in his first text I am sure he did not intend some drunk to shoot up the place.

The Pulse nightclub was a poor example of the point he was trying to make. The Pulse nightclub shooting was a sad day for all when that incident happened. There are other examples of people using guns to stop a mass shooter. Like the one in a Texas church shooting. A man across the street heard the shooting and stopped the shooter.

In the last 20 years there are many examples of an armed bystander that helped prevent further tragedy.

In 1997, the assistant principal of Mississippi's Pearl High School, Joel Myrick, used a 45 caliber semi-automatic pistol to detain a 16 year old named Luke Woodham.

In 2007 Matthew Murray killed 4

people at a Colorado Spring church before being shot by a church member named Jeanne Assam.

In April 2017 an Uber driver with a concealed-carry permit shot a gunman who opened fire on a crowd in Chicago's Logan Square.

In September 2017 an usher at a Tennessee church used his firearm to subdue a masked gunman who killed one woman and injured 6 others.

Note that churches and malls seem to be popular places for these killers.

"*These killers all say they target places where people normally don't carry guns* https://www.creators.com/read/lary-elder/03/18/how-many-lives-are-saved-by-guns-and-why-dont-gun-controllers-care

"Criminologist and researcher Gary Kleck, using his on commissioned phone surveys and number extrapolation, estimates that Americans use guns for defensive purposes 1.2 million times each year and that 1 in 6 Americans who have used guns defensively believe someone would have died but for their ability to resort to their defensive use of firearms."

"...The second point, often ignored, is the very purpose of the Second Amendment. It is to prevent government tyranny through the power of a citizens' militia." "Since 1950, over 98 percent of mass public shootings in the U.S. have occurred in gun-free zones."

Orjan Lundberg. Software engineer, living in Stockholm, Sweden

Case in point that Chicago being gun free.

The left will yell gun control loudest after a school shooting but in New Mexico 11 children were being trained for school shooting according to one report. Yet a Democrat Judge let the 5 adults go on a signature bond. You would think the left would be upset with this crime but very little is heard from them because of Islamic . Siraj Ibn Wahhaj. Brooklyn imam Siraj Wahhaj Sr. is a good friend of the "Women's March" founder Linda Sarsour.

How can we forget the vagina hats and how the left were so upset with Trump locker room talk that they took to the streets with every kind of repulsive reference to a womans vagina. It is like, I am upset that you said that so I am going to repeat it over and over and add to it to create a vile out pouring of vulgar actions that are far worse then a recording that Trump was sorry for. Anyway Linda Sarsour has declared Jihad on our President, and critics. The attack on the NRA is because they have contributed to the Republicans who are all for our Second Amendment. Some say we only want safe guns so they want to take away the scary guns.

Go to this web site to see the states with the most and least gun violence. https://www.usatoday.com/story/ news/nation/2018/02/21/states- most-and-least-gun-violence-see- where-your-state-stacks-up/ 359395002/

Some compare Albuquerque to Chicago

"With the case management order we started to see cases being dismissed by the District Attorney's office and started to see the jail population decrease," Eden said. *"Quite frankly, what I think happened is there were just too many decisions being made in the criminal justice system and that has created a real perfect storm for our state and for the 2nd judicial district."*

https://www.opslens.com/2018/08/21/
new-mexico-Muslim-terrorist-children-
camp/

The New Mexico Muslim Terror Cell
Case Keeps Getting Weirder

by Adam P.

August 21, 2018

According to this article it was a
Democrat Judge Sarah Backus who
ignored warnings from law enforcement
to rule that 4 of the 5 adults in the
terrorist training camp be released on
$20,000 signature bonds. The one adult
of the 5 is being held for kidnapping the
boy who was found dead in a hole where
they lived. People living in a hole
starving and the left does not talk about
this.

A school shooting stopped should be front page news. But because it was a terrorist Islamic group the news is shoved aside so we can talk about the main Trump hate news.

Another way the left justifies their actions against our President is to say "What if it is true." The web site that people show you about the so called Trump lies uses every type of ploy to twist what he says into a lie. They will change history and make fun of him and present their own facts that are lies. Trump was loved and admired before he ran for President against Hillary. He was well known for his altruism and he was given awards for helping people. Such as the Ellis Island Award.

We have all heard that Trump lies. It has been said, "When he opens his mouth a lie comes out."

Now there is a web site called Politifact that has a long list of his so called lies.

If you are in a debate with the other side you need to know the facts. Now in this book you have have facts right at your finger tips. First you will see the tweet then the facts.

Don't be at a loss for words the next time someone on the left tells you how Obama helped this country. I have put in this book how Obama hurt this country and how our President has helped this country. 'Don't be at a lose for words again.

On December 27th,2017 Trump tweeted
"*We have signed more legislation than anybody. We broke the record of Harry Truman.*"
If you go to this website HTTP:// time.com/5081357/Donald-Trump-signed-more-laws-than-Truman/ PolitiFact found this to be true. Later They say he is in last place. One page goes by the first 100 days the other a year. So to make this a lie they changed it to 1 year. Our President had a lot of work to undo the damage Obama did to our country so he did sign a lot of legislations during his first 100 days. Now life is getting better for us and our President's business background is helping us to grow again.

Trump tweets January 30, 2018

"*We enacted the biggest tax cuts and reforms in American history.*

According to BBC news

https://www..BBC.com/news/world-43790895

It is the biggest corporate tax cut in US history.

In the same speech Trump said: "*Our taxes were the highest or among the highest but just about I would say...they were the highest in the world from a business standpoint...*"

BBC news went on to say: "*According to an analysis from the Congressional Budget Office looking at corporate tax rates around the globe in this is essentially true.*"

So our President told the truth.

Tweet

Says Ohio Gov. John Kasich is "very unpopular." August 13, 2018
Politifact will make anything Trump says into a lie.
In March 2011 Kasich was not a favorite among the Ohioans.
Among the Republicans he is not highly regarded according to Herb Asher.
Now among the Democrats he is popular they say but according to the results
If you look at this website you will see why Kasich is unpopular.
www.ontheissues.org/John_Kasich.htm
He has some same views as Republicans
But Politifact makes it into a lie with a poll. Any poll can be manipulated.

ELECTORAL EXPLANATION

There are 3,141 counties in the United State
Trump won 3,084 of them.
Clinton won 57.
There are 62 counties in New York State.
Trump won 46 of them.
Clinton won 16.
Clinton won the popular vote by approx. 1.5 million votes.
In the 5 counties that encompass NYC, (Bronx, Brooklyn, Manhattan, Richmond & Queens) Clinton received well over 2 million more votes than Trump. (Clinton only won 4 of these counties, Trump won Richmond)
Therefore these 5 counties alone, more than accounted for Clinton winning the popular vote of the entire country.
These 5 counties comprise 319 square miles.
The United States is comprised of 3, 797,000 square miles.
When you have a country that encompasses almost 4 million square miles of territory, it would be ludicrous to even suggest that the vote of those that encompass a mere 319 square miles should dictate the outcome of a national election.

On July 16th, 2018 Trump said,;
"The Electoral College is much more advantageous for Democrats."
First off it is important to understand the electoral college and why it is in effect.
As you can see from the Electoral Explanation if we go by the popular vote one or two states could decide the election.
Each state has an allocated number of Electors equal to the number of its U.S. Senators. The Electoral College is made up of 838 electors The Electoral College is put in place to ensure a nation wide system of fairness.
If we relied on the popular vote we would be doomed right now because Hillary would have won.

Now using this map to understand what Trump said we see NY has 29 electoral votes and usually is a Democratic state. California has 55 electoral votes. Our President Trump did not bother with NY and CA but had rallies in Florida and PA. While Hillary was preparing with questions for the debate Trump was having huge rallies.

The Democrats do have an advantage with CA being the largest electoral votes. If Hillary would have won FL and PA at 281 electoral votes then Trump would have only had 257 electoral votes. So it was absolute genius of him to concentrate in FL and PA to win people over. The battle ground states. The Democrats almost always win in Pennsylvania.

The Washington Examiner agrees with our President. With their report in August 27, 2018 called "How the Electoral College favors Democrats and why Republicans must change it" Politifact does not agree and states their opposing opinion. It is clear to me Trump was telling the truth in his opinion.

The next issue ties in with the electoral college one.

Trump stated there's '*substantial evidence of voter fraud.*'

If you say there was voter fraud to the left you will be accused of being a Conspiracy theories. They do not like the facts that there was and is voter fraud going on.

There is so many examples of voter fraud to make this statement true. Green Party nominee Jill Stein had a vote recount. What was found was massive voter irregularities. Even after the voter recount Trump still won. By the way did she return anyones money for the failed recount because she did not make the dead line?

https;//nypost.com/2016/12/14/
michigan-recount-reveals-error-but-not-
the-one-jill-stein-wanted/

In the report 2016 ELECTION
AFTERMATH

By Marisa Schultz December 14, 2016

f"*Republican state Sen. Patrick Colbeck called
the probe a good start on the suspicious
results turned up in Detroit, which Hillary
Clinton won with 95 percent of the vote.*"

The Election Integrity Project of Judicial
Watch analyzed data from the U.S.
Census Bureau's 2011, 2015 statistic
figures provided by 38 states. Eleven
states gave the EAC insufficient or
questionable information.

[2]https://nypost.com/2017/07/14/the -vote-fraud-that-democrats-refuse-to-see

As "*bulletproof evidence of fraud adds up they still claim, 'There's nothing to see here'.*

There are many types of voter fraud.

1.Double voting where an individual cast more than one ballot in the same election. It is hoped that a voter ID card would eliminate this.

2. Voter Suppression which is any tactic aimed at lowering or suppression the number of voters.

3. Voter Registration Fraud. Filling out a voter registration form for a fictional person or a real one without their consent.

4. Dead voter is the use of a deceased person that remains on the voter rolls and a living person fraudulently casts a ballot in that name. Many states like Ohio are cleaning up their dead registered voters.

New York registered voters contained "as many as 77,000 dead people on it's rolls. As many as 2,600 of them have cast votes from the grave, according to a Poughkeepsie Journal computer-assisted analysis.

ON and ON

I think the Democrats do not want to acknowledge voter fraud because most of it is done by Democrats. So Trump told the truth here but you can't get a brainwashed Democrat to admit it.

Here is some more examples of voter fraud

5. Voter Impersonation when a person claims to be someone else when casting a vote in person or an absentee ballot.

There are those that do not want voter fraud to stop so they can stack the votes in favor of a party.

9. Vote buying An agreement between voters and others to buy and sell votes. A candidate pays voters to vote or sell their vote for money.

10. Fraud by Election Officials. Manipulation of ballots such as tossing out ballots.

Ineligible Voter. This can include
non-citizens or felons.

On this I have my opinion that if someone comes into this country illegally they do not know our lows and thus do not have the right to vote. According to the Washington Times STUDY SUPPORTS TRUMP; 5.7 MILLION NON CITIZENS MAY HAVE CAST ILLEGAL VOTES BY Rowan Scarborough June 19, 2017 Some believe non-citizens should have the right to vote but again I say if they do not know our laws and are breaking the law by being here than they should not vote.

This information came from the research organization Just Facts an independent think tank led by conservatives and libertarians.

According to Heritage .org https://www.heritage.org/voterfraud there are 992 Criminal convictions of voter fraud and 48 Civil penalties.

They go on to list each state. A lot are from California

Note that these people have been caught and convicted

And still they blame Russia when in fact it was voter fraud that interfered with our election.

It is a felony to vote more than once in the same election.

Our President tweets

January 30th, 2018

"The immigration visa lottery "randomly hands out green cards without any regard for skill, merit, or the safety of American people."

According to https://www.nilc.org/ issues/workersrights/provworkauth/ *"Since 1986 the immigration law requires employers to only hire workers who have authorization by the U.S. government to work in this country."*

Politifact goes on with how the laws are and that according to the law like everyone out there follows the law in this land.

"*The law requires employers to check (verify) the identity and work eligibility of each employee.*"

It goes on to say that some employers also use E-verify which is a voluntary internet-based program that allows employers to electronically verify the work eligibility of all new hires with the Department of Homeland Security. (DHS) This E-verify can only be used after the worker has been hired. and after completing the jI-9 process.."

OK question if everyone one follows the law why do we have this E-verify and why can they only use it after the person has been hired?

and after completing the I-9 process... [29]
https://travel.state.gov/content/travel/
en/us-visas/immigrate/diversity-visa-
program-entry.html
But why do they need this if everything is
legal. And are there some out there that
do not follow the law so they can hire
cheap labor? There is a saying "Follow
the Money" and I think in this instant
there are business owners that could care
less about America and who want to
make money not looking at the larger
picture of how they are hurting America.

Another news report
https://www.huffingtonpost.com/judy-
frankel/insourcing-american-lose-
_b_11173074.html

Titled

"Americans are losing jobs to foreigners and training their replacements."

Disney laid off 850 American workers and gave some 90 days to train their replacements.

One Disney employee stated that the H-1B workers were *"incompetent"*

"Employers Have Reasons to Abuse Foreign Guest Visas..."

Many take advantage of H-1B workers for the low wage, which save employers billions of dollars.

Again follow the money to get to the crime. The crime being robbing the American people of jobs. Then we have more poor living on the streets because they can't find a job.

"The Numbers of Replaced American Workers are Staggering"

In 2015 the number of visas issued was almost 11 million this according to the statistics at the Foreign Service Posts.

To make Our President into a liar Politifact said "...*He failed to note individuals who come to the United States through the lottery program must be vetted...*" And "*Applicants must meet education or work experience requirements, according to the U.S. State Department and U. S. Citizenship and Immigration Services...*"

Politifact quotes the law and it would be nice if everyone followed the law. There are other factors ...

Politifact goes on to say:
"Donald Trump leaves out facts in claim about visa lottery" Jan. 30th, 2018 by Miriam Valverde

But as you can tell from the previous news report about Disney the workers were not qualified for the job.

The government is suppose to set a cap of 85,000 new H-1B's each year. But there are other types of visas such as:

OPT: Optional Practical Training

F-1: student

B-1: Business 'J-1: exchange visitor

CPT: (Curricular Practical Training) interns who are recruited later.

Q: Special Disney-invented visa for workers who are authentic to the Picot experience.

Then the workers switch to an H-1B.
The switchers are not recorded as part
of the 85,000 cap and there is no way to
check.

The article goes on to say that the
Department of State reports figures for
all 16 different types of work-eligible
visas. When the Government
Accountability Office studied the H-1B
visa program in 2011 they reported
why the number of guest workers were
impossible to track.

So once more Our President told the
truth and Politifact lied.

It was important that they leave out
facts so that they could call our
President a liar.

President Trump stated March 8th, 2018
"*Wages are rising at the fastest pace in more that a decade, something that people have been waiting for about 18 and 20 years. And wages effectively went down. Now, for the first time in a long time, they're starting to go up for people.*"

Politifact stated "*Previously. we rated a similar statement by Trump about rising wages "finally" coming "after years of wage stagnation"*"

Politifact says "Mostly false"
But their little meter shows all false. Then Politifact uses a Federal Reserve Bank of St. Louis graph. Which states the Median real weekly earnings of FULL-Time workers. 1979-2017

I don't like the graphs the left uses to prove their point. If you are going to use a Median earnings graph use a gov graph.
https://data.bls.gov/timeseries/
LES1252881600
use the Change output options boxes to put in 1998 to 2018
The graph shows the Employment rates going up.

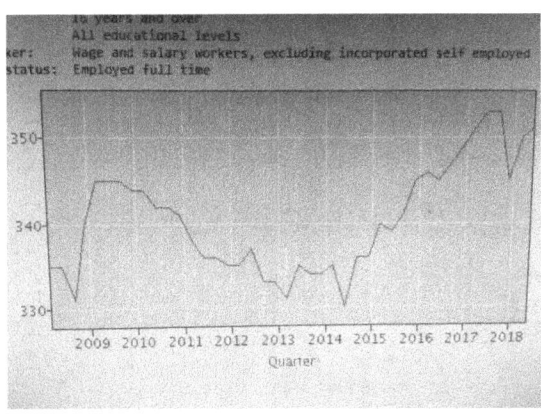

Note again the FULL TIME status.
Lets take what Our President said in
parts.

"*Wages are rising at the fastest pace in
more than a decade...*" So if you look at
the graph and see that wages hit a
low point close to 2005 and have
risen to the highest point we have
had in over 20 years than what
Trump said is true.

The wages for small businesses went
way down because of the
Obamacare.

According to AFF's research ACA (Obamacare) regulations have contributed to at least $19 billion lost wages and 10,000 fewer businesses, and almost 300,000 lost jobs. Small business could not afford to pay for health care. Some had to cut peoples hours back to defer the cost.

Another AAF study showed the hotel industry suffered sense the National Labor Relations Board's 2015 decision to "broaden the joint employer standard. In 2016, following the NLRB decision, the franchise employment growth in the hotel industry slowed to a greater significant extent. Even in 2017 the hotel franchises were still struggling.

https://www.NLRB.gov/cases-decisions/weekly-summaries-decisions

You can use this web site and type in 2015 to see what they are talking about.

Not only were hotels upended but the direct or indirect standard reduced the incentive to franchise.

Evidence showed that the 2015 standard instantly damaged industries that relied on franchises.

You can read more at https://www.americanactionforum.org/insight/nirbs-new-joint-employer-decision-means-labor-market/#ixzz50wX9ue9v

Many have said that Obama was responsible for the economy changes for the better but that simply is not so. When President Trump overturned the NLRB's 2015 "*ambiguous direct or indirect control joint employer standard*" it was a relief for franchises, their workers and the labor market. If the Democrats take back the house they could reinstate the old standard that hurt the franchise business.

Many small businesses were glad that the GOP won on repealing and replacing Obamacare. Health care was a source of pain for many small-business owners.

I have discussed this issue with many on the left and their answer was that small businesses should supply health care. A small business can't afford to pay for health care. I watched many small businesses shut down in my town and I am sure all across American they shut down because of Obama care. Now that Trump is our President I am seeing more open up and prosper. So basically if you can't afford ObamaCare then there is job loss.

A new tax law that lowered the corporate tax rate from 35% to 21% will help millions of hard working Americans pay their bills and enjoy their lives.

https://www.usatoday.com/story/opinion/2018/02/21/small-businesses-booming-under-trump-tax-cuts-gary-rabine-column/340627002

The left attack our President when ever he tells how the economy is growing by saying that it was because of what Obama did. They all repeat this lie as a rebuttal but it simply is not so. Bottom line is undoing what Obama did is what is helping our economy grow.

Thursday, December 28th, 2017 in a NY Times interview Our President said;

"Dianne Feinstein said "there is no collusion" between the Trump campaign and Russia.

https://www.youtube.com/watch?v=0BS5amEq7Fc

A CNN video where the caption under the video reads;

"Dianne Feinstein said "there is no collusion" The Washington Free Beacon published May 4th, 2017

The commentator asks Dianne Feinstein *"Do you have evidence that there was in fact collusion between Trump associates and Russia during the campaign?"* Dianne Feinstein answers, *"Not at this time."*

Politifact that hangs on every word
writes that she said "Not so far." So
they lied because she really said, "Not
at this time." See it works both ways.
The Mueller investigation has gone
off into left field so it is no use
expounding on the old Russia
collusion waste of time.

Moving right along
"Hillary Clinton lied many times
to the FBI."
— *Donald Trump on Monday,
December 4th, 2017 in remarks to
reporters*

**Donald Trump falsely claims
Hillary Clinton lied to FBI**

*By Miriam Valverde on Tuesday,
December 5th, 2017 at 9:00 a.m.*

They go on to say that James Comey told Congress there was "no basis to conclude she lied to the FBI."

Comey has been fired because he hurt the FBI's reputation. He mishandled the Clinton email investigation.

n fact Hillary lied to the FBI 4 times. I was looking up some written article that Hillary lied to the FBI and came across this Politifact web site of Hillary Clinton lies. https://www.politifact.com/personalities/Hillary-Clinton/statements/byruling/false

If the FBI asked questions that were
very guarded so that she could get
away with her crime and go on as a
candidate for President then
according to Comey she did not lie or
have intent to do any wrong. The left
does not like to talk about Hillary and
will say that she was tried and not
guilty of the email crimes.

I found an article from Politics
"Clinton Ally Aided Campaign of GBI
Official's Wife" By Devlin Barrett
dated Oct. 24, 2016 The Wall Street
Journal.

"The political organization of Virginia Gov. Terry McAuliffe, an influential Democrat with longstanding ties to Bill and Hillary Clinton, gave nearly $500,000 to the election campaign of the wife of an official at the Federal Bureau of Investigation who later helped oversee the investigation into Mrs. Clinton's email use."

https://www.wsj.com/articles/clinton-ally-aids-campaign-of-FBI-officials-wife-1477266114

This could be called Pay-For-Play

The Hill article called "Pay for Play is the Clinton way."

by Rick Manning dated 8, 24,2016

In this article we find this little nugget of truth about Russia.

"For the "what difference does it make" crowd, you can no longer credibly claim that Bill Clinton's half million-dollar honorarium (as reported in the New York Times) for a speech in Russia was not tied to the decision that followed shortly thereafter to allow many of the same Russian actors to gain control of 20 percent of the U.S. uranium reserves"

So basically if the FBI was very careful in questioning Hillary and worded in such a way as to make her statements seem factual then they can honestly say she did not lie to them.

Yet on you tube we have videos of Comey being questioned
When Comey was questioned in the Congressional Oversight Committee admitted that Hillary lied. But the question is did she lie to the FBI.

CBS News
Published on Jul 7, 2016
SUBSCRIBE 891K

Rep. Trey Gowdy questioned FBI director James Comey during a House Oversight Committee hearing into the FBI's investigation of Hillary Clinton's email practices as secretary of state. Gowdy was the chair of the House investigation into the Benghazi attacks, which first uncovered Clinton's use of a private email server.

Just because she lied to the American people does not mean she lied to the FBI if they were careful in what they asked her." So this one is a toss up if we believe what Comey said.

As a final end to this book what many do not know is there is a coup to impeach Our President. The Media is working with George Soros's to do just that. So there is a Coup D'etat against Trump and the MSM is working daily on this. If you see news that says "This may be true." or "If this is true." that means there is no facts to back up what they are reporting. That is a ploy of the MSM enemy of the people.

Explanation of the front cover.

Top is the code found on the Q page turned sideways.

The men standing in a line are much like the Matrix men who stood before Neo. Left to right Clapper, Acosta, Rosenstein, Soros in the middle of it all, Mueller with an overly large head,Obama looking very angry, Cooper the Albino, Lemon looking evil.

ON the left stairs in Agent Smith suits are Comey, Maddow, and Stelter. On the right Mudd, Cuomo, and Strzok.

The room is a room of the White House. They are trying to take the White House. President Trump is protected by the Shield of Truth.

Back cover Matrix word saying Trump tells the truth Media lies.

www.ingramcontent.com/pod-product-compliance
Lightning Source LLC
Chambersburg PA
CBHW070340290526
45791CB00003B/1404